FULL VOLUME

POETRY
A Scottish Assembly
Sharawaggi (with W. N. Herbert)
Talkies
Masculinity
Spirit Machines
The Tip of My Tongue
Selected Poems
Apollos of the North

ANTHOLOGIES
ed., *Other Tongues: Young Scottish Poets
in English, Scots, and Gaelic*
ed., with Simon Armitage, *The Penguin Book of Poetry
from Britain and Ireland since 1945*
ed., with Mick Imlah, *The New Penguin Book of Scottish Verse*
ed., with Meg Bateman and James McGonigal,
Scottish Religious Poetry
ed., *The Book of St Andrews*

CRITICISM
The Savage and the City in the Work of T. S. Eliot
Devolving English Literature
*Identifying Poets: Self and Territory in Twentieth-Century
Poetry*
The Modern Poet
Scotland's Books: The Penguin History of Scottish Literature
ed., *Robert Burns and Cultural Authority*
ed., *The Scottish Invention of English Literature*
ed., *Heaven-Taught Fergusson*
ed., *Contemporary Poetry and Contemporary Science*

FULL VOLUME

Robert Crawford

CAPE POETRY

Published by Jonathan Cape 2008

2 4 6 8 10 9 7 5 3 1

Copyright © Robert Crawford 2008

Robert Crawford has asserted his right under the Copyright, Designs
and Patents Act 1988 to be identified as the author of this work

First published in Great Britain in 2008 by
Jonathan Cape
Random House, 20 Vauxhall Bridge Road, London SW1V 2SA

www.rbooks.co.uk

Addresses for companies within the Random House Group Limited can be found
at: www.randomhouse.co.uk/offices.htm

The Random House Group Limited Reg. No. 954009

A CIP catalogue record for this book is available from the British Library

ISBN 9780224080873

The Random House Group Limited makes every effort to ensure that the
papers used in its books are made from trees that have been legally sourced from
well-managed and credibly certified forests. Our paper procurement policy can
be found at: www.rbooks.co.uk/environment

Typeset by Palimpsest Book Production Limited, Grangemouth, Stirlingshire
Printed and bound in Great Britain by
William Clowes Ltd, Beccles, Suffolk

for Alice, Lewis, and Blyth

with love

I'm truly sorry Man's dominion
Has broken Nature's social union

Robert Burns

CONTENTS

ADVICE

When you are faced with two alternatives
Choose both. And should they put you to the test,
Tick every box. Nothing is ever single.
A seed's a tree's a ship's a constellation.
Nail your true colours to this branching mast.

YIN AND YANG

after Paz

In my body you scour the sgurr
For its sun buried deep in the forest.
In your body I search for the boat
Let slip in the middle of the night.

BRONZE AGE

Fights and kisses, touch and go,
Body-heat and cool, wedding-day downpour,
Tin yin fused to the yang of copper,
I want our Bronze Age to last forever.
If simple, it would all be over.

THE CHANGE OF LIFE

Sometimes full volume is a breathy whisper.
'There's something I need to say.' You tilt your ear

Towards love's ensuing, lifelong pent-up silence
Crackling with all you want, but fear to hear.

SATNAV

In this windy town of lamps and horizons,
Corbels and kissed, martyred stone,
Where broadband flits down slim, carved vennels,
Sunlight projecting pinecone shadows
Under the water of the lade,
At the end of a leyline that runs forever
Past playing-fields at Canongate Primary School
Where all the clauses are linked by cartwheels,
At the very centre of this off-centre town
We come together, lost and found.

LOCAL

The global village doesn't mean the globe
But somewhere like that warm pub in St Andrews
We kissed in before seeing on television
How all the chemicals that make our bodies
First emigrated here from far, raw stars.

A GEAN TREE

At the Botanics,
late,
I stand under, I understand
a gean tree, suddenly,
Kyotoishly
eyeing its
blossoms at night, its
white
lamplit flutter
by my mouth –
petal on petal
not grown
up root and branch, more
levitated
or flounced down
from stars, a damp
nebular dance, a drifted
spring manna
here
not yet landed
where each of us
with thanks
must take our time.

WRITER

The fields bleached
Pristine with frost;
The ridges rumpled;
Ptarmigan,
Pale, living flakes of snowcem
Flaked from Our Lady of the Braes;
Thick grasses fletched
Against quick clouds;
Fat, matted sheep;
A winter hare's
Powdery kick; the bare
Silver birch, the fir
Needled with ice;
Your hair
A little greyer now
Year by year:
I carry each back
To the black loch, the loch of ink.

PRETENDER

The lie I live is different from yours.
I will be true to it until I die,
Faithful forever to the trompe l'oeil truth
Of the bee-orchid or the fishing fly.

SHETLAND VOWS

I swear by the unfallen broch of Mousa,
I swear by fallen Snarravoe on Unst

That it is possible to rise above them
Over the rainbowed green nub of The Knab,

And sense, way out at earth's circumference,
Sceptical London, Laramie, Hong Kong

Who doubt the arctic tern-packed broch of Mousa
Or Snarravoe on Unst are as they are,

But, knowing such disbelief, go on believing
In voes and fluff, in monuments and rain

Below the wing's pale rind, and keep faith both
With the soaked planet's whole revealed horizon

And with home ground, the national smudge of Scotland
That holds my wife, our daughter, and our son.

SAME, DIFFERENCE

for Kay

Since each is shaped
by all its drift,
by every updraft
from high cloud to ground,
in all the history of the world
a snowflake's double
can't be found.

Since each is shaped
by all its drift,
by every updraft
from snowflake to ground,
in all the history of the world
a high cloud's double
can't be found.

A world of difference flecks each word.
Nature abhors a Henry Ford.

A DAY'S WORK

A day's work
is never done.
It's dawn
always somewhere,

time to clot
a hole with leaves,
to scar and scour
clay,

to let a river
drift
and lift
its bed away,

or sky a stone
upright
or fly
between sheets

of rain,
and touch
down again,
reach

out and along
the same strong,
shaped, reshaped
new ground forever.

ROUNDING

Fast in the tides' flow
Each day rough boulders, rounding,
Wear away oceans.

Oceans wear away
Boulders each rough day, rounding,
In the tides' fast flow.

CRANNOG

A coppiced alder, Baba Yaga hut
On fowls'-leg stilts, deep-silted in a loch,

Ringed by lost swansnecked cloak pins, overboard
Jet beads, and long-unyelled-for hazel hurdles,

Built with built-in surround-sound sound of wavelets
Dawn to dusk to dawn. Every day

Its being shifts with the wind.
To walk to it you have to walk on water

Bridged with hewn wood. Inside thick, wool-stuffed walls
Cloudberry nibblers, scavengers for sloes,

Inhaled strewn bracken, kindled mouse-nest tinder
And focussed on the fire, as we do now

In this one replica among the many
That once stood here, their slim-poled absences

Stinging our reverent, underdeveloped
Sense of quickened water, wind, and hearth.

CHORUS

It was a bad sign when the sung
Ballads were written down
So one rich man might own
A people's songs;

And now I've heard that at Cornell
There's a recorded hoard
Of cries of extinct birds.
If earth is ill

And local sights and sounds will drown,
Still dawn downloads again
Freely for everyone
Uncosted song.

CEMETERY

Anon

Our lips are sealed.
Our language now is murmured
Nowhere above ground.

Teacher

The traditional
Gaelic inscription translates,
'Not enough wild sex'.

Librarian

All flesh is grass, but
I hope also to become
A yellow iris.

Priest

Friend, when you read this,
Bear in mind without a doubt
There can be no faith.

Deer

In death as in life
Breathless and isolated
I run with the herd.

Bottle

I saw it happen.
I could not stop it. Always
I wept through one eye.

Telephone engineer

I connected up
Wet, remotest villages;
Let their sounds carry.

HONEY

after a Gaelic lyric in the Book of the Dean of Lismore

Honey is the call of any bird;
Honey a human voice in the Land of Gold;
Honey a crane's song, and there is a heard
Honey Bun Da Threoir's waters hold.

Honey is the calling of the wind;
Honey the cuckoo's voice above Caise Con;
Honey in uncluttered, random sunlight,
Honey blackbirds' songs till sunset's gone.

Honey the eagle's cry at the Red Falls
Way above the Bay of Morna's Boy;
Honey the cuckoo's call beyond the thickets;
Honey is that pause in the crane's cry.

My father Finn MacCoul had in his war-band
Seven squadrons ready to fight any
Man or beast; when we unleashed the deerhounds
They leapt ahead, their baying pure wild honey.

KISS

For want of a mountain a primrose was lost,
For want of a primrose a love song was lost,
For want of a love song a sly kiss was lost,
And that was the thing that mattered most,
Yes, that was the thing that mattered most.

NEAR AUCHTERMUCHTY

High in treetopia, on the treetop walk,
I stare straight down the thick trunk of a beech,

Its brontosaural hoof splayed in the earth.
Whirligig beetles, roe deer, fang-eyed wolves

Animate Fife's farflung woods and ponds.
Carnbo to Carnbee the pollen blows,

Scumbled with light. Walking up here, breezed on,
Eye-to-branch with sycamores, alert

To downdrafts or the slipstream of a squirrel,
I let my mind fill with yon falconer

Shouting and shouting to a blank blue sky
Until at last, just as he knew it would,

The Harris Hawk comes from its other world
Beyond the human eye, senses his calling,

Stoops, and disappears back into view.

FULL VOLUME

Diving-suited, copper-helmeted, no thought of turning
    back,
Led by his grey lead boots way, way off the beaten track,

He walks into Loch Ness. His unheard wife and daughter
Stand hand-in-hand on the shore. Underwater,

He ploughs on down on his own, bone-cold marathon,
Stomping the loch not for any sponsorship he's won,

Not seeking front pages, nor getting caught up in some
    blinding
Damascus flash, but just for love of that dark, reminding

Him and his folks here and all the folks
Back home that, despite the old jokes,

Hoaxes, photos, no-shows, and tourists' tales,
Something is in there, out there, down there, flails and
    dwells

In inner silence. He wants to meet
It, to come back dry, dripping, and greet

The day from the loch's beyond, its call
Calling inside him. Wants above all

To sound the loch's full volume right at ground
Level, be lost in it, pushed by it, sung by it, not to be found.

TIR NAN OG

after Pessoa

What is the sea voice deeper in the waves
Than simply the voice of the sea?
It is a voice that calls
But, if we listen, falls
Silent because we listen too intently.

Only if sometimes in a kind of dwam
We hear, oblivious to what we hear,
Then it can speak and keep
Alive in childlike sleep
A hope that makes a dormant smile appear.

That island in the firth is Tir nan Og,
Stretching unmappably,
Where the King waits, apart
In hope, but if we start
To wake, silence. Only the sea.

A CANADA

It was spring
When the boat came
From nowhere, though you could hear,
Miles off, the skirl of pibroch
Rallying ice-cliffs
Around the lake,
One brother rowing,
The other piping
Like a figurehead
At a dory's prow.

You never saw them
All through the winter.
They ferried spring, though,
One talking hunting
While the other drank.
At the trading post
Leather-kneed locals
Heard words like *siubhal*
And praised those brothers
For the airs they played.

All that was way back
Not where I live now
But at a lake north
Of Memphramagog
We moved away from
When I started school.
I still remember
That year no spring came,
Just a single rower
In a silent boat.

OMENS

after the Gaelic of the Carmina Gadelica

Monday at 6 a.m.
I heard a lamb,

And then, while I sat by,
A snipe's kid-cry.

I saw the cuckoo, grey as slate,
Before I ate.

On Tuesday, late,
A slimy flagstone shone
Where snails had gone,

And the wheatear, like
Ash off a dyke,

Flapped where the old mare's black
Foal stumbled and turned its back.

I sensed right there,
Right then
            a right bad year.

AFTER GAELIC

Listening, in the Monadhliadhs
Or by lochsides in Nova Scotia,

You can still crawl along on your belly
Through a secret commonwealth of elves and fairies

Lost among shitake mushrooms;
Inch like a stalker or an Inca hunter,

Imitating the common earwig
Forficula auricularia,

Ear to the ground of a Gaelic drove road
Before it gives way to the bypass.

CLAN DONALD'S CALL TO BATTLE AT HARLAW

after the Gaelic of Lachlann Mór MacMhuirich (fl. 1411)

You Clan of Conn, remember this:
Strength from the eye of the storm.
Be at them, be animals,
Be alphas, be Argus-eyed,
Be belters, be brandishers,
Be bonny, be batterers,
Be cool heads, be caterans,
Be clashers, be conquerors,
Be doers, be dangerous,
Be dashing, be diligent,
Be eager, be excellent,
Be eagles, be elegant,
Be foxy, be ferrety,
Be fervid, be furious,
Be grimmer, be gralloching,
Be grinders, be gallopers,
Be hardmen, be hurriers,
Be hell-bent, be harriers,
Be itching, be irritants,
Be impish, be infinite,
Be lucky, be limitless,
Be lashers, be loftiest,
Be manly, be murderous,
Be martial, be militant,
Be noxious, be noisiest,
Be knightly, be niftiest,
Be on guard, be orderly,
Be off now, be obdurate,
Be prancing, be panic-free,
Be princely, be passionate,

Be rampant, be renderers,
Be regal, be roaring boys,
Be surefire, be Somerleds,
Be surgers, be sunderers,
Be towering, be tactical,
Be tip-top, be targetters,
Be urgent, be up for it,
In vying be vigorous
In ending all enemies.
Today is for triumphing,
You hardy great hunting-dogs,
You big-boned braw battle boys,
You lightfoot spry lionhearts,
You wall of wild warriors,
You veterans of victories,
You heroes in your hundreds here,
You Clan of Conn, remember this:
Strength from the eye of the storm.

COMING TO FRANCE

*after the Latin 'Adventus in Galliam' of George Buchanan
(1506–82)*

Badlands of Portugal, bye-bye
Forever, starving crofts whose year-round crop
Is lack of cash. And you, fair France, bonjour!
Bonjour, adoring sponsor of the arts,
Your air's to die for, and your earth's so rich
Vineyards embrace your warm, umbrageous hills,
Cows crowd your pastures, glens gabble with burns,
Broad, open meadows fan out fields of flowers;
Sailboats go gliding down long waterways,
Fish throng your ponds, lochs, rivers, and the sea
Where, left and right, your harbours greet the world
With open arms. Unstinting, smiling France,
Your towns are stunners, safe, walled, turreted,
Sights for sore eyes, stacked out with shining roofs;
Your folk are never pushy, but plain-speaking,
Well dressed, well-fed, so ready to be friends.
France, *alma mater* of the universe,
Faithful, happy, flourishing at peace,
Jocund and easy, but grim-faced in war,
Unbeatable, but not flushed with success.
When the going's tough you show true grit. You stand,
Defender of the true faith, with no time
For foreign bigots' fads. Well-balanced France,
Your summer's free from arid heat. Your winter
Gives up its bleak excesses at your hearth.
No east wind plagues make autumn faces pale,
No spring floods drown your farms with fast-thawed ice.
France, if for just one instant in my life
I cease to love you as my *patria*,
Send me straight back to Portugal's dour badlands,
Those crofts whose only crop is lack of cash.

HENRI CARTIER-BRESSON

Before and after
He buried his Leica
When the Nazis
Took him away
He still remembered
How to shift perspective
By a slight bending of the knees.
He went on learning
Through the bearded man,
Hand held, palm up,
In the Warsaw Ghetto;
Through the deathcamp child
Standing with a badly rolled umbrella,
That though the saying goes, *Seeing is believing*,
Believing is also seeing;
And he found too
Through the cowboy weeping,
Through the youngster
Doing a handstand
In the road,
How everything human
That has ever happened
Happens in the blink of an eye.

THE EAR

Locust Street
Was his first locus,
Cicadas singing
Through carless nights,

And in the distance
God-given gifts
Of ragtime
To a shy, white boy

Reading by lamplight
On windless evenings,
Crisp turning pages'
Tace et fac

As the big river
Went on forever
Articulating
Without a word

Where the Missouri
Joins the Mississippi,
Their waters swelled there
By the Illinois,

Late drip-drop raindrops,
A coal fire's crackle,
No airconditioning
Conditioned him.

All explanation
Is mere evasion,
In the end only
The ear is sound.

THE ALSO RAN

The hare wasn't there. The hare was nowhere
To be seen, a sheen
Of kicked-up dust, the hare's coat,
Every hair of the flank of the hare so sleek, so chic,
It was sponsored, it caressed his physique.
Out of sight, out of mind, the unsponsored tortoise fell
Into a vertical sleep that sank him deep
Down in his shell. He dreamed. He smelled the smell
Of formula one. The stop, start
Of his own heart slowed on the chicaned road
To hibernation. He dreamed station
After station flew past the filmy blue
Carriage window of dwam, his shell a bullet train
Trained to hurtle, to startle, but with tortoise feet,
Not wheels, not rails making the beat,
Beat, beat of speed. He felt torque eat
All of him, call to him, willing him, through him
Birling the earth. A surge, a rebirth
Hurried him on. Each hour, each day
Rushed further away. As he slept, stock still,
Every path, track, hill, housing estate, landfill
Site, every dawn, noon, night
Shot past faster, a happy disaster, a true
Gift of the gods, a one-off, out of the blue,
Till waving children, doe-eyed does, sped past
Ahead of sound, and the tortoise thought earth might
Out-accelerate light, the planet's race, pace, place
In the universe changing. Then, ranging
Further than any dream has ever gone,
The tortoise shone. A comet. A meteor. Shone,
His shell a re-entering rocket, a capsule straight down like a stone
From outer peace. Och, plunged in the innermost space
Of the dream, he was sure he had lost, and so sure he had won

In his way, and would have his day, the Spring Day
Of the Slow Start. He played his part
Well. He sang his dream and in the spring its claim
On his listeners grew. They knew, like you
And I, it was true.
Even the hares, when they heard what he said, stopped dead
Inside themselves, beside themselves, stunned
At how the tortoise seemed to have gunned, to have shot
From the starter's pistol by staying stock still. They thought
It was great, it was cool. They loved
How he hadn't moved but the earth had sped beneath him.
They were with him. When he sang, they sang along,
Whiskering, whistling his song. And the tortoise, sleepy,
    wiser,
Let them sing. And the hare? He was nowhere. A survivor
Off in a puff of dust, but in the huff
That sharper, tougher, fitter, leaner, thinner,
He was only the winner.

THE EVENING STAR

from the Greek of Sappho

Hesperus, ferrying home all bright dawn scattered,
You ferry home the sheep, you ferry home the goat, you
    ferry the child home to mother.

WYOMING

for Blyth

Up on a ridge
Near Rogers Canyon,
Two centuries
Since it was made,
My daughter dances
In a teepee ring
Where she sees some
Of what they saw –
Wind-whetted grass,
Elk heading south.
The prairie shines
As she looks round,
Fingering a honed,
Sharp, greenish stone,
Not an arrowhead
But the flint from which
One once was chipped,
The stone that stayed
So the same stone could fly.

MEASUREMENT

Nine and Seven, one by one,
Lay face down on a home-made skateboard,

Hauling it forward, inch by rope inch,
Into the Tomb of the Eagles.

Seven glissaded down Maes Howe's
Five-thousand-year-old chute,

Walked unbowed through its entrance passage
Whose stone slabs weigh forty-five cars.

Nine chased Nine with dog-track speed
Round Orphir's circular kirk,

Dropped down rung after midnight rung
Metres into Wideford Hill.

Nine and Seven bounced and drummed
On the capstone over Brough of Birsay's

Pictish well, where a jeweller made silver leaves
Decades before the Norse sauna.

After the sun this winter solstice
Does its light work in between

The low hills of Hoy, then Nine and Seven
Will never be sixteen again.

BIOLOGY

for Lewis

Our days and ways, our chromosomes are numbered,
Lettered, making up a long, tagged story,

A still unfolding Book of Genesis,
But one, like poetry, lost in translation,

So most of us, to find the original sense,
Must call to mind some song our mother sang,

One taken in with nursery rhymes and milk,
Then dream we come to love strange dialects –

From *zymogens* to *Avogadro's number* –
Whose folktales speak in strands of narrative,

Dense, trailing clauses scribbled by pipettes,
Enzyme legends, each a secret pathway

Through tiny mitochondric organelles,
Where carnitine, the label proteins read,

Acts out unseen, wee recognition scenes,
Atom-fine get-togethers, microbondings,

Pos and neg held in a cyclic shape,
And there, in trees, in cats' or human kidneys,

Articulates a sort of Word made flesh,
Goes recognised, unspoken, joins together

Mice, people, choughs, so colourlessly proving
Gut feelings true, that all are held in one

Genetic myth, one Loch Ness-deep, compelling,
Deft, intermolecular embrace.

BROADBAND

Search engines crawl
The cloned net, combing
Each pixeled word
In that bright
Etruscan light,
That web of heaven
Which seems to cost
Nothing,
Where the lost
Are found
Spellbound
At their screens,
Every question
Surprised
By its answer,
And smells are dumped
Offline, in the sump
Of earth below,
This swirl of snow
And rain we live in
Where
Bees desert their hives
And our rushed lives
Dwindle into mobile phones
And though we're all
On our last warning
To clear the air,
To pay
As we go,
Today
I still
Don't know
What to do

Except to pray
No human ear
Will ever have to bear
The world's full volume.

EMPIRE

Everywhere now is Tenochtitlan
Now Tenochtitlan is gone,

Its diorite pumpkins, grasshoppers carved from cornelian
Looted to far-flung museums.

The net, the web, pitches the world
Towards technopolitan Tenochtitlans,

Endless Aztec digital empires
Where each is captured, migrated, held –

Even that hypnotic, caged
Puma in Montezuma's zoo,

Gleaming chest rising and falling
In digitized, black-bristled sleep.

REALLY

Hi I'm Lois I'm lonely I live near the motorway on Lewis
Want to chat with me? I love chatrooms
You might have seen me on TV I'm really feral I'm twenty-one
I love chatrooms Want to chat with me?
It's so hot here I love Paris I used
To dance there I've just washed all my hair Hi
I love Existentialism Want to chat with me?
I temp as an archaeologist but mostly do modelling
I love ballooning and bathyscaphing
I've lots of piercings I love liquefied oxygen
My parents think I'm too young to be a field marshal
I love chatrooms Want to chat with me?
Don't you think logarithms are really depraved?
I love chatting with other teenage girls
I love power-tools and petrol-driven saws
I've just been skinnydipping Hi I love chatrooms
My favourite film is *The Sound of Music*
I live in a cage of iron and glass Want to chat with me?
I love ballet and labanotation Hi
I'd like to invite you It's so hot here
I've been making lots of aluminium
I need to shower I love chatrooms
From my bedroom window I can see lots of Swedish people
I get really excited about geodetic surveys
Ever done one? Want to chat with me?
I've got this cool new theory of colour
I'm really lonely I miss China I've a secret tattoo
Next year I'll be sixteen Want to chat with me?

HAIKU

From that first email
We were living together,
Late, migrating swans

Winging it, crossing
Iced firths' spliced noons and midnights,
Messaging, apart,

In that otherworld
Where we met when we emailed
There is no other

You are my question
In that fingertip waiting
You are my reply

THE DIGITAL LIBRARY,
ST ANDREWS

for Alice

Here in Scotland's oldest bookhoard
Used since the Middle Ages,

From secret seams of inked enlightenment –
Wanlockhead Miners' Library,

Or that jewel inlaid in the fields of Perthshire,
The reading-room at Innerpeffray –

How many hops, skips, and jumps
To the right conclusions it took to slip

Into this tip-tap Aladdin's-Cave-
Cum-stormed-Bastille, this free-for-all

Where laptops open like thick-leaved books
The flatpack wealth of nations.

THE EXORCIST

after the Latin 'Franciscanus' of George Buchanan (1506–82)

A barren haugh. No flowers, no trees for miles.
No use for harvest. Barbed-wire thistles spatter
Dour, poisoned fields. Bare space. Hoofprints of cows.
Dysart, folk call it. Under desert earth
Vulcan's mile-long unmined coal still smeeks
In runnelled caves. Random, lung-clogging fires
Belch out all over through the veins of rock,
Firing up flumes of fumes, and, underfoot,
Pica-fine, pitch-black clouds smother the soil.
Jailed in dark caverns, sheer heat tries to burst
Up through drab, crusty, perforated ground
All over, fissuring that tired-out waste,
Reeking of sulphur. Father William Lang,
Franciscan spin doctor to James the Fifth,
Let on that he could hear lost souls being racked there,
Could tune in to their endless yells and yowls
And spot dark demons wildly trampolining,
Slewing their sinewy tails across the beach.
One day in Dysart on an empty stomach
He said he breathed the low cuisine of Hell.

So, after spinning this tremendous story,
Lang decks himself out as The Exorcist,
Scrawls an enormous circle inside which
Other much smaller circles are sketched out,
And drives a stake, dead-centre; plonks beside it
A crackling cauldron. Then, all mumbo jumbo
And last-gasp oaths, he stirs in salt and ashes.

Act Two. The Reverend Holy Father Lang,
Dressed to the nines, goes ladling holy water
All round, and, hocuspocussing like mad,
Denounces devils, then invokes the heavens,
Earth, firth, and all Acheron's bowel-dark kingdoms
Rifting and belching in the deepest depths.

Act Three. The Dark Night of The Sacred Secrets.
Hordes of local farmers crowd around:
Wives, husbands, nubile daughters come to gawp,
Itching to see what's up; but, just in case
They catch him out, Lang yells, 'Stand back! STAND BACK!
Especially you who have not made confession
Since yesterday, or else these trepidatious
Phantoms may flit before your uncleansed presence,
Or Cacodaemon with his greasy jowls
Gulp you right down and flense your sin-drenched shanks!'

Act Four. A local yokel, The Boy Martyr,
Is hauled out to the stake. He knows Lang's game,
But still he's shit-scared, just as if, about
To jump blithely ashore from Charon's ferry,
He catches slobbering Cerberus chomp up
The bodies of the damned. Maybe his granny's
Stories come back to haunt him, or it's just
That carbon copy of hell's kitchen-stink,
Dysart's midnight pitch-black darkness, spooks him.
The farmers cower. The exorcism goes on
With no one except Lang having a clue,
Though everybody hears groans, grumbles, voices
Threatening, then chanted prayers, answers
Flung out to questions nobody had asked.
One moment bowing to the dirt and beating
His chest, the next his eyeballs rolling round,
Lang goes for broke, and hoses holy water

All night, till the dawn chorus scares away
One last ghost way down to his ancient den.

Act Five. The folk go home. Lang cites as true
What no one really knows: the spirit's fate;
The bushfire heat of purgatorial flames;
How many pots and pans hell's demons stir;
How many souls they skewer on their spits;
How many souls get drowned in waves of ice;
How many masses it may take to let
Each soul off just a bit; it sounds as if
Lang wrote the Rough Guide to the Underworld.
His audience loves it, and soon Purgatory's
Back in fashion, much to Martin Luther's
Disgust – and Purgatory's hoary glory
Would still be mushrooming, had it not been
For Lang's wee sidekick who, whether through fear,
Or for a bribe, or after one too many,
Spills all the beans – that Sorcerer's Apprentice,
That sad debunker of The Exorcist!
From then on all the hopes of Dysart shrivel.
Nothing can bar the Glory of the Truth.

So take heed after this not to make up
Fake phantoms, spooks that hoof it through the night,
Tales of the Unexplained, unless of course
They take place far from home, way out among
The Spaniards or the Coimbran Portuguese,
Or way, way out in Dark America,
Or underneath the Ethiopian sun,
Where no eye-witnesses can say you're wrong,
Or where the Nile's source hides out in the desert
And no one knows the Dysart Exorcist.

COOLED BRITANNIA

Prime Minister Tony Blair's Farewell Speech to his Native Land

for Robert McNeil

The hour approaches. Check your fly.
It's almost time to do or die.
All Scotland knows England expects
No independence. Sacred texts
Are trotted out: *Neighbours, Macbeth,*
Our glorious canon. Pale as death,
Balmoral royals and chat-show stars
Kneel in House of Commons bars;
Great Britain falters, all at one
As if arranged by Trevor Nunn,
Piously praying, 'Let Union last
Long as Lord Reith, or Ossian's ghost!'
Forget those loans, forget Iraq –
I was the one won Scotland back!
Aye, now's the day, and now's the hour!
Vote! Vote! Remember Brown and Blair!

O comrades queueing from Unst to Luss,
Just make your wee St Andrew's cross.

47

WOOL AND WAR

after the Latin of Florentius Wilson of Elgin (c. 1500–47)

Never mind our European allies.
The Arab snuggles into wool. It's worn
By peoples round the delta where the Nile
Courses down from sky-high mountain peaks,
Splashing broad fields each year, slashing across
The desiccated soil of Libya
In one grand arc. Upscale designer dressers
Sport wool in old Damascus, and so too
Does the Cilician youngster when not bathing
In sparkling Cydnus. Thracians love to wear
Pure wool. Wool clothes alike the freeborn West
And those ruled by that Scythian dictator
To whom our own failure to stand united
Has handed all the empire of the East.
Now, though, to build on foreign policy
Disasters, we're rearming, summoning
That tyrant over here to blitz our cities
As if we gave our enemy a sword
And begged, 'Now, stab me, stab me in the guts.'
These days, ignoring our true interests,
We fight among ourselves, ready to wage
A dirty civil war. Our shared beliefs,
Our closest allies' manifest defeat,
The burned-out shrines of the true God – all fail
To make us act. Religion has been wrecked.
Artists are exiled. Everywhere today
The enemy is winning. Times to come
Will see through all our tears and arguments,
Rhetorics of tyranny and empire,
Hunger and blood till, time and time again,
Posterity will curse the warmongers

Who started this, who first failed to confront
The coming dangers and to stop the madness
Right at the start. These arms, these men, they'll say,
Ignored the spirit. We chose to screen out
Just what they were after all along.

DALRIADA

Praise to physics, praise to song,
He chanted as he strode along
Cathcart Street in the Greenock heat
Of summer 1939.

The gramophone and science books
Stoked up his dreams. He hoped to fuse
Ships' engines, Gaelic, firth, and sky
In a Greenock choral symphony.

My mother liked that man. He lay,
Flung from a bike whose brakes had failed,
Near West Loch Tarbert, on his way
To take a schoolboy to a fair.

The boat that brought his body back
Slowly from Campbeltown was called
The *Dalriada*. As it sailed
Round past the Cloch, men at the rail

Stood silent, hatless. Soon a Blitz
Changed that small world. Miss Millar, back
From bramble-picking near Dunoon,
Found all her street and family gone.

I heard her in her sleep once call
Their names; so I speak this for her,
Hugh Roberton's Orpheus Choir, and all
The hopeful singers of that ancient kingdom.

DOORSTEP

I can still smell him. T. L. Essiott,
Pin-thin reviewer in his gloomy flat
Under that tube station at Marble Arch.

A rasp and clank of passing trains above
Made dark slicks dribble from his lidless Quink
Across the sea of papers on a rolltop.

His hall was lined with unoiled cricket bats
Autographed by Novelists' Elevens
From Oxbridge colleges. Shelved on the walls

Taxidermied heads of minor poets
Mixed with Virginia's toothbrush, Ezra's cufflinks,
A spattered sunshade that had sheltered Proust.

Standing at his front-door, I could hear
Trains make a ziggurat of empties clink –
Probably that Paraguayan whisky

He'd christened Essiott's Rocket Fuel because
It could accelerate him towards a deadline
At ninety words a minute, which he runed

In Linear B shorthand, then typed up
On his smashed Remington. Its juddery ribbon
Had been changed, once, by Arthur Conan Doyle.

I never saw him eat. He lived on liquids,
Literary gossip, cigarettes.
Lunch must have been a bun thieved from some launch.

This was the literary life. His adverbs
Asphyxiated Yale. His bad reviews
Could axe whole Faculties. One good would save

Lives, marriages, and sales of foreign rights.
He looked me in the eye. He cleared some phlegm
And spat it on his doorstep. 'Well. Come in.'

BELEAGO

after the Latin of George Buchanan (1506–82)

Diogio de Murça, Head and King,
Rector of Coimbra University,
We all admire the way you've got ahead,
But your Sub-King Co-ordinator of
Commercialisation, your Head of Advanced, Enhanced
Entrepreneurship, that wee
Master Beleago, MBA
(Monster of Bestial Accumulation),
Whose ugly hooves tramp on our heads
Is so pigheadedly convinced
That he has wholly Mastered Being Ahead
Of us, your mere human resources, he
Goes and sells off everything: sells goats,
Sells pigs, sells cattle, killing
Whole herds so he can sell and sell;
Birds of the air, fish of the sea –
He sells the lot: your pears and nuts,
Plums, peppers, reconditioned cucumbers
Grown in your labs, your onions, garlic,
Capers and corianders sprouting
In students' grassy gardens – all for sale.
Dead magpies marketed as pheasants' breasts,
Goats' meat as mutton, broken bones jammed in your
    mince.
Lord Rector, Head of Coimbra's School,
Show us a better way to get ahead
Than that Belial-bellied Beleago,
Our no-brain, blackballed Baal of the Unbelles Lettres
Of Marketing, our Mall-mad Manager,
For what he says he possesses he doesn't possess,
What he says he professes he can't profess,

Iago-Beleago, Shylock of Market Stalls,
Server-up of venison sludged from pigs' balls,
Thrice winner of the Nobeleago Prize
For out-Cretaning Cretans with his Courses in Creative
    Lies,
Cretinous silly-git syllogist, philosobutcher, Zeno of Lard,
Exhibitionist, inquisitionist, circumcisionist,
Throatslitter, nestshitter, brainquitter, inkspitter, Grand
Inquisitor's Portuguese Libyajewish Supergrass who grassed
Me up, got me arrested, tested, tortured, chucked
In prison, that Magog of goats and groats,
That Papal brown-noser, that Sniffer-out-of-Heretics-in-
    his-own-Sandals,
That academic Vandal, I want to hear him caught and
    locked and trapped
In his own echoing 'Sell! sell! sell! sell! sell! sell!'
Forever, so I can sing
Your praises, Lord Rector, and pray
With a loud shout, a whoop, a from-the-heart 'Wey-hey-
    hey!' –
Baal-Iago, Beleago, BYE BYE!

EYES DOWN

Today I wake like a chainsawed forest,
Snuggled in my limitations.

Not for me The Bigger Picture;
More the blurred, peripheral vision

Of a couple muzzy after love.
Intent on my toecaps, I've glimpsed the blue,

Gullied surprise of gentians in deep frost,
Budapest tramlines bronzed with chestnuts,

Everywhere an eyes-down planet
I would have missed if I'd been looking up.

THE KIRK

Good for directions, creeds, and mysteries
Of blood-bead, mustard seed, bread, water, wine,

You're part of the horizon in our midst,
Skymark and landmark, take-off point, and stark

Terminal building where, at start or finish,
Some seek the spirit like a mislaid passport

To daily light, or past the Milky Way's
Communing disc of otherworldly stars;

Some live God's sums of plenitude and loss,
Christ on the cross and then the Christless cross;

Some hear the seasoned Word clear as a bell;
And some, an inch, a clinch, a world away,

Touch and discover what it is to love
The carved wall of a church that's without walls.

MADONNA AND CHILD OF THE BULLFINCH

State University of New York, Binghamton

Here he is – the dandled, laptop Christ
Tugging on a string incised on gold

Tied to dark claws. You see again
The way the focused eye of faith could see

In this Renaissance painting red and black
Centuries-old feathers flying blind

With zip-code neatness back to Mary, and Jesus
Who's not let go. You hear how, through the snows

Of New York State, it homes with a whistlebinkie's
Died-and-gone-to-heaven rush of song.

*whistlebinkie: literally 'bench-whistler', a Scots word meaning a
spectator who has not contributed a gift to a wedding and is left to
sit and whistle for his own amusement*

WALKING THE PLANK

Someday it must be done: walking the plank,
Braving the spectacle of vertigo,
Strolling in good faith it will be easy
To hop aboard a ship at the other side.

BIO

in memory of Colin Matthew

I, day.

I, crinoid. I, bristle-worm. I, Goliath beetle.

I, moss. I, orb spider. I, magnolia. I, wobbegong.

I, spurge hawk moth. I, thallus. I, water. I, cyathozooid. I, horseshoe crab.

I, pink flower mantis. I, swallowtail. I, prairie dog. I, locust. I, capercailzie.

I, manta ray. I, rattlesnake. I, sycamore. I, manatee. I, honeybee. I, saddleback. I, lamprey.

I, coelocanth. I, okapi. I, salmon. I, snapper. I, fire. I, anolis lizard. I, orchid. I, tree frog.

I, iguana. I, ant. I, skink. I, sidewinder. I, archaeopteryx. I, hoatzin. I, heron. I, king penguin.

, saddle-billed stork. I, bird of paradise. I, cormorant. I, bower bird. I, macaque. I, cassowary.

darter. I, armadillo. I, marmoset. I, bluebell. I, humpbacked whale. I, possum. I, spruce. I, sequoia.

bbon. I, zebra. I, wild dog. I, chimpanzee. I, sloth. I, wallaby. I, Washingtonia. I, pearly nautilus.

on. I, tupaia. I, ptarmigan. I, skunk. I, brachiopod. I, dolphin. I, bear. I, dachsund. I, koala. I, chiwawa.

mpire bat. I, vole. I, silverfish. I, hornet. I, camelia. I, panther. I, chipmunk. I, primrose.

nnosaurus rex. I, crown-of-thorns starfish. I, argus pheasant. I, human. I, chameleon. I, stick insect.

t. I, thorny devil. I, Portuguese man o' war. I, moon rat. I, flying fish. I, blue-footed booby. I, ferret.

rrow. I, lion. I, komodo dragon. I, thistle. I, yucca moth. I, stratocumulus. I, cicada. I, apatosaurus.

apo. I, dipper. I, tapir. I, gurnard. I, segmented worm. I, Venus' flower basket. I, tiger. I, stork. I, microbe.

allee fowl. I, hummingbird. I, macaw. I, dragonfish. I, hawkmoth. I, jaguar. I, impala. I, caecilian.

sea-horse. I, swimbladder. I, orang-utan. I, Douglas fir. I, pipa toad. I, woodpecker. I, air. I, wryneck.

, baboon. I, parakeet. I, horse. I, hedgehog. I, protistan. I, weasel. I, great crested grebe.

I, mushroom. I, hydrogen. I, limpet. I, flying fox. I, hammerhead. I, mudskipper. I, brittle star.

I, pig. I, gecko. I, gannet. I, axolotl. I, tortoise. I, solenodon. I, python. I, parrot.

I, toucanet. I, monkey-puzzle. I, oxygen. I, hyena. I, gourami. I, springbok. I, moa.

I, ichthyosaur. I, daffodil. I, buzzard. I, impala. I, numbat.

I, albatross. I, cat. I, liverfluke. I, slug. I, lancelet. I, hesperornis.

I, crocodile. I, vervet monkey. I, salamander.

I, night

NOTES ON THE VERSIONS

'Yin and Yang' is a version of Octavio Paz's 'Comple-mentarios', though it also departs from it. It uses a line and takes guidance from Eliot Weinberger's translation, 'Counterparts', in his parallel-text edition and translation of Paz's *Collected Poems:1957–1987* (Carcanet, 1988).

'Honey' is a version of the Gaelic lyric 'Binn guth duine i dTír an Óir' which I found in Neil Ross's parallel-text edition of *Heroic Poetry from the Book of the Dean of Lismore* (Oliver and Boyd for the Scottish Gaelic Texts Society, 1939) where it is attributed to Oiséan Mac Finn (Ossian). 'Honey' is reprinted from my *Scotland's Books: The Penguin History of Scottish Literature* (Penguin, 2007).

'Coming to France', 'The Exorcist', and 'Beleago' are versions of Latin poems by George Buchanan drawn from my paral-lel-text *Apollos of the North: Selected Poems of George Buchanan and Arthur Johnston* (Polygon, 2006) which gives full details of the poet and records my debts to several Latinists.

'Tir nan Og' is a version of Fernando Pessoa's 'As Ilhas Afortunadas' which I found in James Greene and Clara de Azevedo Mafra's parallel-text *The Surprise of Being* (Angel Books, 1986); it is guided by their translation.

'Omens' is a version of the Gaelic 'Manaidh' which I found in Alexander Carmichael's parallel-text *Carmina Gadelica, Hymns and Incantations, Volume II* (Oliver and Boyd, 1928); it is guided by the translation there.

'Clan Donald's Call to Battle' is a version of the Gaelic poem beginning 'A Chlanna Cuinn, cuimhnichimbh' which is reprinted in Carolyn Proctor, *Ceannas nan Gàidheal/ The Headship of the Gael* (Clan Donald Lands Trust, 1985). I am grateful to Meg Bateman who read the poem aloud to me and discussed it. The version in this book is reprinted from my *Scotland's Books: The Penguin History of Scottish Literature* (Penguin, 2007).

'Wool and War' is a version of Florentius Wilson's 'Laudes et Commoda Insulae Britanniae', which I found in the third volume of William Duguid Geddes's *Musa Latina Aberdonensis* (1910), and is guided by his prose summary.

ACKNOWLEDGEMENTS

I am grateful to the editors of the following magazines where some of these poems have appeared: *London Review of Books, Oxford Poetry Broadsheets, Poetry, Poetry Review, St Leonard's Church Newsletter, Times Literary Supplement, Yale Review.* Other poems appeared in the Scottish Poetry Library anthology *The Thing That Mattered Most: Scottish Poems for Children* and in my books *Apollos of the North: Selected Poems of George Buchanan and Arthur Johnston* (Polygon, 2006), *Contemporary Poetry and Contemporary Science* (Oxford University Press, 2006), *and Scotland's Books: The Penguin History of Scottish Literature* (Penguin, 2007). Thanks to BBC Radio Scotland for commissioning several of the poems for 'Night Email', a programme made with Bill Paterson and produced by David Stenhouse; other poems were broadcast on Radios 3 and 4 in programmes about George Buchanan produced by Dave Batchelor and Louise Yeoman. For advice and hospitality in connection with the writing of some of these poems, I would like to thank Meg Bateman, Alex Cluness, Caroline McCracken-Flesher and Paul Flesher, Rona Ramsay, Bruce Richardson, the Shetland Arts Trust, the T. S. Eliot Society of St Louis, the University of Wyoming, and Yale University.

This book was completed during dreamtime funded by the Arts and Humanities Research Council and the University of St Andrews.